Close to the Wind

The Beaufort Scale

Peter Malone

G. P. PUTNAM'S SONS

I would like to thank the Meteorological Office, Exeter,

the National Maritime Museum, Greenwich,

and the Royal Naval Museum and HMS *Victory* at Portsmouth

for their assistance in the researching of this book.

G. P. PUTNAM'S SONS

A division of Penguin Young Readers Group. Published by The Penguin Group.

Penguin Group (USA) Inc., 375 Hudson Street, New York, NY 10014, U.S.A.

Penguin Group (Canada), 90 Eglinton Avenue East, Suite 700, Toronto, Ontario, Canada M4P 2Y3 (a division of Pearson Penguin Canada Inc.).

Penguin Books Ltd, 80 Strand, London WC2R 0RL, England.

Penguin Ireland, 25 St. Stephen's Green, Dublin 2, Ireland (a division of Penguin Books Ltd.).

Penguin Group (Australia), 250 Camberwell Road, Camberwell, Victoria 3124, Australia (a division of Pearson Australia Group Pty Ltd).

Penguin Books India Pvt Ltd, 11 Community Centre, Panchsheel Park, New Delhi - 110 017, India.

Penguin Group (NZ), Cnr Airborne and Rosedale Roads, Albany, Auckland 1310, New Zealand (a division of Pearson New Zealand Ltd).

Penguin Books (South Africa) (Pty) Ltd, 24 Sturdee Avenue, Rosebank, Johannesburg 2196, South Africa.

Penguin Books Ltd, Registered Offices: 80 Strand, London WC2R 0RL, England.

author or third-party websites or their content. Published simultaneously in Canada. Manufactured in China by South China Printing Co. Ltd.

Design by Marikka Tamura. Text set in Bernhard Modern. The illustrations were done in watercolor and gouache on hot press watercolor paper.

Library of Congress Cataloging-in-Publication Data

Malone, Peter, 1953–

Close to the wind : the Beaufort scale / Peter Malone. p. cm. 1. Beaufort scale—Juvenile literature. I. Title.

QC931.4.M35 2007   551.51'80287—dc22   2005032672   ISBN 978-0-399-24399-8

1 3 5 7 9 10 8 6 4 2

FIRST IMPRESSION

All places mentioned herein are real places. To the best of my knowledge none of the ships existed nor any of the characters

with the exception of John Smeaton and, of course, Francis Beaufort himself.

In memory of my uncles,

Bob Malone and Eric Evans, who found themselves at the sharp end of naval history,

and Martin Malone, who spent a considerable part of his U.S. merchant marine experience on the *Tusitala*,

one of the last commercial square-riggers.

Plaque from Beaufort's house in Manchester Street, London

The Beaufort Scale

On the first of July, 1810, Captain Francis Beaufort of the Royal Navy entered into his journal a carefully graduated scale for measuring the force of the wind, a scale he began developing in 1805. Beaufort's purpose was to provide mariners with a clear and precise means of classifying and recording weather conditions at a time when instruments to measure wind speed did not exist. His observation-based system offered sailors a way to rank the winds they encountered and gave them a common language to share those observations. Beaufort's original scale did not have wind speed, but listed a set of qualitative conditions from 0 to 12, by how a naval vessel or a man-of-war would act under them. Zero meant too calm to sail and twelve meant a wind stronger than any canvas could withstand.

Beaufort's scale was officially adopted by the Royal Navy in 1838, and became mandatory for naval log entries. Although the scale was adapted over the years for differing circumstances, Beaufort's central idea of defining weather conditions through observation remains—and it still works. Across the world, shipping forecasts still use those selfsame numbers written in July 1810 in the captain's cabin of HMS *Blossom*. That, surely, is Francis Beaufort's lasting achievement.

In the following pages you'll see a nautical journey experienced by a typical midshipman during the time of Beaufort. All the places mentioned herein are real; the characters, except, of course, for Francis Beaufort and engineer John Smeaton, are fictional.

Peter Malone

CALM.

SEA SURFACE: sea like mirror.

EFFECTS ON LAND: smoke rises vertically.

MAN-OF-WAR will be becalmed.

William Bentley

" 16 July 1805.

Dear Lizzie—

Six months to the day since leaving Portsmouth

and we are becalmed so long at Naples that I am turning Italiano! The harbour

can scarce be less hot than the rumbling guts of the volcano, old Vesuvius himself.

Every morning it is a regular little floating market full of everything you'd want,

and plenty you wouldn't. We have orders to sail as soon as enough breeze presents

itself. If only! . . ."

—Letter home to his sister from midshipman William Bentley
on board His Majesty's Ship *Zephyr* of 36 guns.

stem

T he *Zephyr* is as old as William (12),
but at 156 feet from stem to stern,
151 feet longer.

stern

LIGHT AIR.

SEA SURFACE: ripples with the appearance of scales; no foam crests.
EFFECTS ON LAND: smoke drift indicates wind direction; vanes do not move.
MAN-OF-WAR with all sails set will just have steerage way.

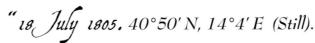

" 18 July 1805. 40°50' N, 14°4' E (Still).
Two bells forenoon watch. This morning there is a hint of a breeze
from the North-East, and the ship is to be checked and readied for sea,
should it prove to blow any stronger."

To the ancient Greeks, Zephyr was the god of the west wind.
When the ship was named after him, it was forgotten that in his
youth he enjoyed making hurricanes and causing mayhem at sea.
However, later in life Zephyr mellowed and was known
as the bringer of soft breezes and spring flowers.

So why is the figurehead a female?
Maybe the man who carved it thought that *Zephyr's* crew
(all 261 of them)
would be cheered up by having a lady on board.

LIGHT BREEZE.

SEA SURFACE: small wavelets; crests of glassy appearance, not breaking.
EFFECTS ON LAND: wind felt on face; leaves rustle, vanes move.
MAN-OF-WAR will sail at one to two knots.

Elizabeth Bentley

" *18 July 1805. 40°50' N, 14°4' E (for the last time!).*
Dear Lizzie—

Hurrah! Finally enough wind to shake the sails, up anchor and leave Naples.
And my first command—I am given charge of the jolly-boat to fetch two
of our stragglers from the quayside."

In 1759 a British engineer called John Smeaton
devised a scale for measuring wind on the basis
of how fast the sails of a windmill seemed to
turn. William's father has two such mills
on his farm, which grind wheat into flour.
It can therefore be said that both he
and his son depend upon a good breeze
to do their business.

William's father's windmills

GENTLE BREEZE.

SEA SURFACE: large wavelets; crests begin to break; scattered whitecaps.

EFFECTS ON LAND: leaves and small twigs in motion; wind extends light flag.

MAN-OF-WAR sails at three to four knots.

20 July 1805. 39°48′ N, 11°30′ E.

Letter to Lizzie posted at Gibraltar 8 days later.

"Dear Lizzie—

I have found this poem by Mr. Thomas Gray:

> *'Fair laughs the morn, and soft the zephyr blows,*
> *While proudly riding o'er the azure realm*
> *In gallant trim the gilded vessel goes;*
> *Youth on the prow, and Pleasure at the helm; . . .'*

My very situation not ten minutes ago, on our own 'prow,' surrounded by dolphins leaping and diving, though I ain't exactly sure I'd call the bo'sun Pleasure! . . ."

The bo'sun

From the Baths of Agrippa, Rome

The Greeks and Romans regarded dolphins as creatures of good fortune. They were said to save drowning sailors, to transport souls of the drowned to the afterlife, and like the albatross, to bring misfortune and bad luck if killed.

MODERATE BREEZE.

SEA SURFACE: small waves becoming longer; numerous whitecaps.

EFFECTS ON LAND: dust, leaves and loose paper raised up;

small branches move.

MAN-OF-WAR sails clean and full at about five or six knots.

"24 July 1805. 37°28' N, 1°49' E.

We are sailing well with the wind on our larboard quarter;

the studding sails have been set to increase our speed.

When the bo'sun was below deck we dared each other to walk along the main yard,

fifty feet up and as thick as the cook's waist, an activity at which Maybrick excels.

I am sure that he is half ape and will prove to have a tail."

The speed of a ship is calculated in knots or nautical miles. This is measured by dropping a rope over the stern that is attached to a reel. At the dropped end of the rope is a piece of wood known as the "chip," and along the rope, knots are tied at intervals of 47 feet, 3 inches. The chip remains in the water behind the ship and the knotted rope will unwind from the reel for thirty seconds, measured by a sandglass. The faster the ship is moving forward, the faster the rope will unwind. The number of knots passing overboard during this time is the speed of the ship.

This is what four knots looks like.

FRESH BREEZE.

SEA SURFACE: moderate waves taking longer form; many whitecaps; some spray.

EFFECTS ON LAND: small trees in leaf begin to sway.

MAN-OF-WAR will carry optimum sail.

" *28 July 1805, Gibraltar.* 36°7′ N, 5°22′ W.
A few days ashore before facing the Atlantic. Up to the top of the Rock to watch ships working through the straits, view Africa, and feed the monkeys. Relatives of Maybrick?"

It is not known how the monkeys, the only colony in Europe, arrived on Gibraltar. Myth says Hercules, but they were probably brought by the Moors.

However soft or hard the wind blows, it does not always come from the ideal sailing direction. If the direction of the ship is at a slight angle to wind direction (2), a greater expanse of sail can be engaged than if the wind is directly behind (1). However, if the wind is too much from the side (3), the other side of the ship will push against the water, causing resistance and slowing the ship's progress.

If the wind is head-on, the ship must attain its destination by zigzagging in a series of maneuvers called tacking. Even so, the wind must remain behind the fully braced sails shown in (4), in order for the ship to move forward.

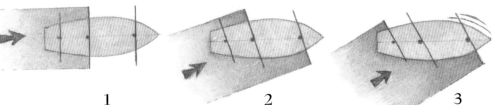

1   2   3

4

STRONG BREEZE.

SEA SURFACE: larger waves forming; whitecaps everywhere; more spray.
EFFECTS ON LAND: larger branches of trees in motion; difficulty with umbrellas.
MAN-OF-WAR will have single-reefed topsails and topgallant sails.

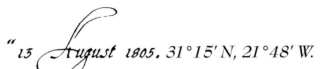

"13 *August* 1805. 31°15' N, 21°48' W.
*We are a week out of Gibraltar and attend our daily sextant class on
the quarter-deck. The North-Easterly on our starboard quarter blows us
along nicely, and has made an offering of Maybrick's hat to Neptune.*"

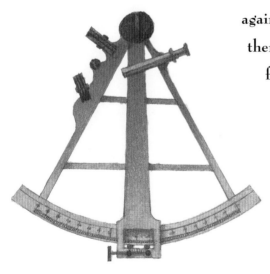

A sextant is used along with astronomical almanacs, nautical charts and a very
reliable type of watch called a chronometer to give the ship's position according to
latitude and longitude. This is usually done by measuring the angle of the sun at noon
against the horizon. Midshipmen are highly trained in all areas of seamanship to qualify
them as officers. Navigation is particularly important; the sea's a big place with very
few features to recognize, so knowing where you are at any given time is crucial.
They are also expected to have practical knowledge of the tasks performed by
ordinary seamen, such as going aloft, which means climbing way up the masts.
Zephyr's main mast is a towering, stomach-churning 148 feet high. Nerves of
steel and the agility of a monkey are essential at sea.

NEAR GALE.

SEA SURFACE: sea heaps up; white foam from breaking waves begins to blow in streaks.

EFFECTS ON LAND: whole trees in motion; difficult to walk against the wind.

MAN-OF-WAR will have double-reefed topsails and topgallant sails.

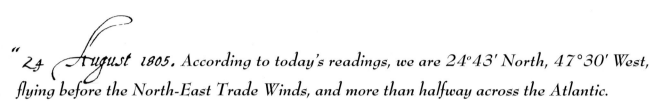

" *24 August 1805. According to today's readings, we are 24°43' North, 47°30' West,*
flying before the North-East Trade Winds, and more than halfway across the Atlantic.

> *'A wet sheet and a flowing sea,*
> *A wind that follows fast*
> *And fills the white and rustling sail*
> *And bends the gallant mast; . . .'*

If it blows any harder, we'll be striking the topgallant masts. Already a second reef in the topsails."

Taking in reefs is a way of making sails smaller as wind increases (too much wind can tear sails, part rigging and even break masts and spars). Reefing points are loose ropes arranged in lines at the front and back of the sail that are tied together over the yard, in a reef knot, to achieve this. The sailors in the picture to the right are tying a second reef into the fore and main topsails. This is a complicated procedure, as are most others on ships like the *Zephyr*, depending on teamwork and each man knowing his allotted task.

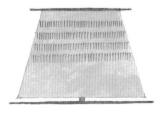

Unreefed

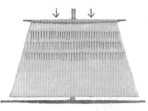

Single reefed

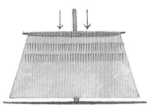

Double reefed

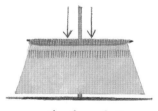

Triple reefed

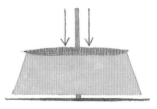

Fully reefed

GALE.

SEA SURFACE: moderately high waves of greater length;
edges of crests begin to break into spindrift; foam is blown into well-marked streaks.
EFFECTS ON LAND: twigs and small branches broken off trees; walking made difficult.
MAN-OF-WAR will have triple-reefed topsails, jib and courses.

"30 August 1805. 18°20' N, 57°40' W.
Blowing harder today. Weatherside main tack parted at five bells, first watch.
Clewed up to yard for new rope."

That there is such a thing as a maritime dictionary should come as no surprise. The language of the sea is as colorful as it is baffling. Sailors also mark the time of day in a manner wholly unfamiliar to landlubbers. Each day "begins" at noon, and is divided into five watches of eight bells' duration (a bell equals half an hour), and two watches of four bells.

Like their originators, some figures of speech found their way ashore from time to time and formed part of everyday parlance, such as

"three sheets in the wind"—drunk;

"sailing close to the wind"—pushing one's luck;

"took the wind out of his sails"—put him in his place, and

"I don't like the cut of your jib!"—I don't much care for the expression on your face.

STRONG GALE.

SEA SURFACE: high waves, seas begin to roll;
dense streaks of foam; spray may reduce visibility.

EFFECTS ON LAND: slight structural damage occurs;
slates and chimney pots dislodged.

MAN-OF-WAR will have close-reefed topsails and courses.

"1 September 1805. 16°26' N, 61°40' W.
The wind has shifted North and we have not come upon as favourable
a passage through the Leeward Islands as we had hoped for.
We are obliged to pass close to a French port and fly their flag
as a ruse to avoid unwelcome attention from their guns."

For an age with a more pronounced sense of honor than our own,
it is curious that the deception of flying someone else's flag was
an accepted aspect of naval warfare. The shift in the wind's
direction is due to a storm that, though some way to the east,
is relentlessly gaining on the ship. French gunnery is the least
of the *Zephyr*'s problems; many times more sailors die by
shipwreck than by enemy action.

STORM.

SEA SURFACE: very high waves with overhanging crests; sea takes
white appearance as foam is blown in very dense streaks;
rolling is heavy and visibility is reduced.
EFFECTS ON LAND: trees broken or uprooted; considerable structural damage occurs.
MAN-OF-WAR will scarcely bear close-reefed main topsail and reefed foresail.

"*2 September 1805. 15°20' N, 62°40' W. Wind shifted North-West.
The master, who's sailed these waters many times, says it's a hurricane, and that
we haven't felt the worst of it yet. There is now no chance of reaching Jamaica,
and our best course is to run South-East before the wind, and get ourselves
as far as we can from the storm's center.*"

A great deal of activity precedes a storm at sea.

Topgallant masts and yards and studding-sail booms are detached and sent down
to be tied on the skid beams next to the ship's boats. Lifelines are set out upon deck
for clinging on to and the guns lashed to their rings in a variety of different ways.
Rigging and steering gear are checked and prepared against breakage.

As many as four men will be working the wheel
to stop this sort of thing from happening.

VIOLENT STORM.

SEA SURFACE: exceptionally high waves;
sea covered with white foam patches and visibility still more reduced.

EFFECTS ON LAND: widespread damage.

MAN-OF-WAR will reduce sail to storm staysails.

"*3 September 1805. 14°5' N, 61°30' W. Wind West-North-West and fearful strong.
Waves like houses. We are scudding South-East, the wind astern and two points to starboard.
The wind moans, hums and shrieks as it whips through the rigging, nothing will stay dry and
the pumps work in relay. No galley stove these past two days, so cold meat and ship's biscuit
for them as can keep it down. Misery and terror. Still, calm seas never made skillful sailor.*"

Hurricanes in the Caribbean usually move west; heat and moist air provide the energy to start and maintain
their circular motion. Within the storm the wind revolves inward and counterclockwise (clockwise in the southern
hemisphere), increasing in velocity toward the center. Watch the water draining from a bathtub, and you can
observe a similar effect. You might also notice that at the very center of the plug hole there is no water, and
that it appears to be pushed back to the sides. This is also true of a hurricane, where there is a still center called
an eye in which there is no cloud, and wind speed drops to ten knots or so.

The wind is greatest in the northern half of the hurricane. Although the *Zephyr*
is comparatively fortunate to be in the less violent southern half, the wind is still
very strong and the decision has been taken to carry more sail than is correct
in order to reach the storm's edge as swiftly as possible.

Course of
Hurricane

Course of HMS. Zephyr.

HURRICANE.

SEA SURFACE: sea completely white;

air filled with foam and driving spray; visibility still more reduced.

EFFECTS ON LAND: widespread damage and devastation.

MAN-OF-WAR will carry no sails.

3 September 1805. Same date. 30 miles east of last reading. Apart from some pieces of mast and rigging, there is no sign of HMS Zephyr. The wind is from the west and Zephyr the god has returned to buffet and cause havoc with his namesake.

Most sailors would have infinitely preferred an engagement with the enemy than an encounter with a storm at sea. In a fight, at least one is preoccupied; there is no prospect of prize money in a brush with a hurricane. Those not required to do what was absolutely necessary on deck were below coping with the situation as best they could—avoiding injury through falls, working the pumps in relays, standing by with axes to clear fallen rigging, spars and masts, and hoping for the best.

Letter from William to his sister, 6 September 1805, Bridgetown, Barbados, 13° N, 59° 30' W.

"Dear Lizzie,

It was a dashed near thing that we've been through, a full blown hurricano that came close to overwhelming us, and indeed succeeded in carrying away our mizzen topmast and main topsail. It took great effort to clear the wreckage and jury-rig a replacement the following day, at the end of which we reached Bridgetown, the wind mostly gone but with a great swell upon the sea. A most singular occurrence—yesterday I found a spring flower upon the deck which I have pressed and enclose for you . . ."

The Zephyr limping into Bridgetown

The Fate of Some Ships

It is remarkable that any ships survive from Beaufort's time. HMS *Victory*, Nelson's flagship at Trafalgar (1805), remains a commissioned ship of the Royal Navy, and still flies an admiral's flag, albeit from her berth in a dry dock at Portsmouth. The frigate *Trincomalee*, built of teak in Sri Lanka in 1817, was recently restored after many decades as a Royal Navy training vessel. The USS *Constitution*, "Old Ironsides," is probably the oldest ship afloat.

After their active life ended, some ships suffered the ignominy of becoming floating prison hulks before their final trip to the breaker's yard. Such was the fate of the *Bellerophon*, the ship to which Napoleon surrendered after his final defeat in 1815. The timbers of others, such as HMS *Beagle* and USS *Chesapeake*, became parts of buildings. Other ships were sold to Castles', manufacturers of garden furniture, who broke up old ships and turned their oak into benches and the like. They had this remarkable building on the Thames at Westminster, decorated with their victims' figureheads.

About 1,800 oak trees would be needed to construct the hull of a ship such as the *Zephyr*. The sides could be up to twenty-one inches thick, to offer some protection from enemy fire.

Tall straight pine trees provided wood for the ship's masts. However tall a pine may be, it alone is not large enough to become the mainmast. This was made from a number of trees lashed together and bound with iron hoops. The mainmast of the ship shown at right would be about ninety-two feet long.

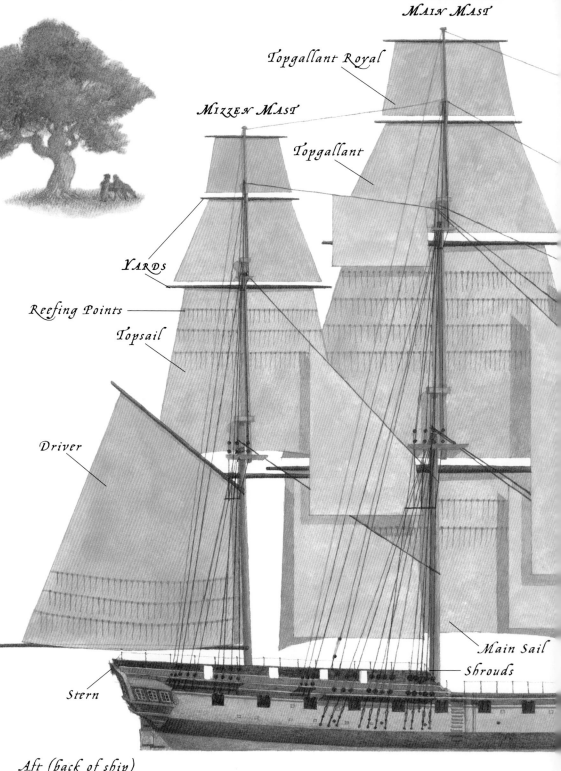

MAIN MAST

Topgallant Royal

MIZZEN MAST

Topgallant

YARDS

Reefing Points

Topsail

Driver

Main Sail

Shrouds

Stern

Aft (back of ship)

A late eighteenth century man-of-war, such as HMS Zephyr

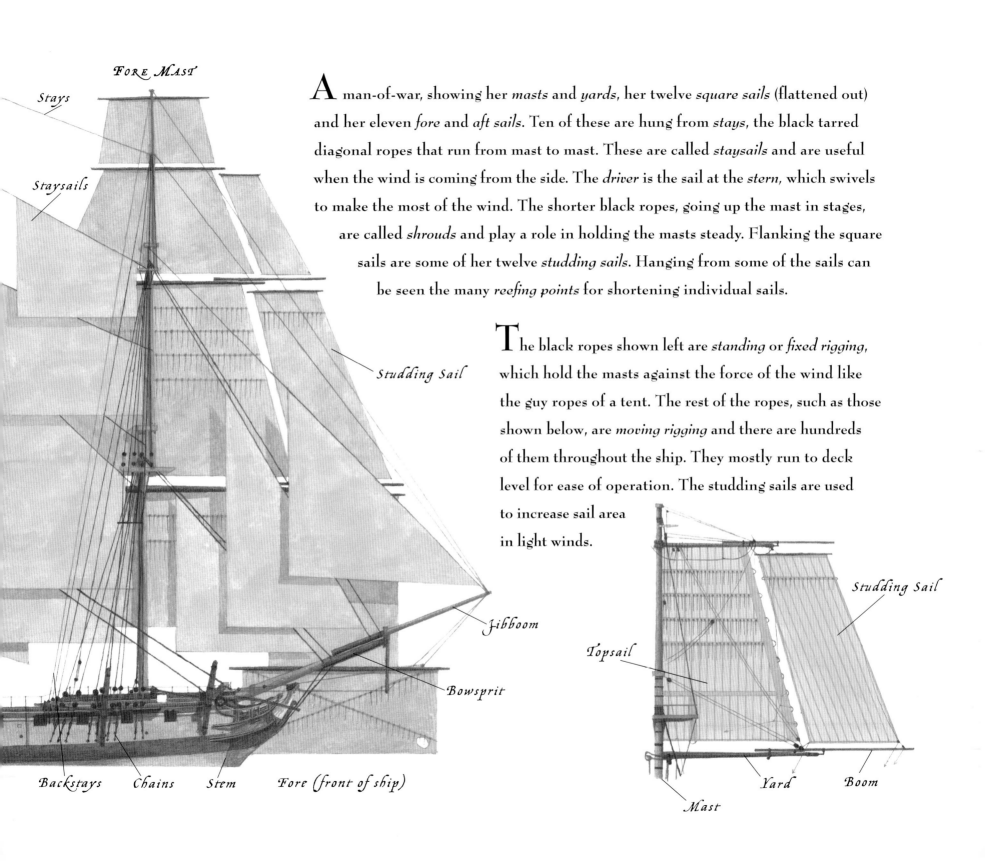

FORE MAST

Stays

Staysails

Studding Sail

A man-of-war, showing her *masts* and *yards*, her twelve *square sails* (flattened out) and her eleven *fore* and *aft sails*. Ten of these are hung from *stays*, the black tarred diagonal ropes that run from mast to mast. These are called *staysails* and are useful when the wind is coming from the side. The *driver* is the sail at the *stern*, which swivels to make the most of the wind. The shorter black ropes, going up the mast in stages, are called *shrouds* and play a role in holding the masts steady. Flanking the square sails are some of her twelve *studding sails*. Hanging from some of the sails can be seen the many *reefing points* for shortening individual sails.

The black ropes shown left are *standing* or *fixed rigging*, which hold the masts against the force of the wind like the guy ropes of a tent. The rest of the ropes, such as those shown below, are *moving rigging* and there are hundreds of them throughout the ship. They mostly run to deck level for ease of operation. The studding sails are used to increase sail area in light winds.

Studding Sail

Topsail

Jibboom

Bowsprit

Backstays Chains Stem Fore (front of ship)

Mast

Yard Boom

WILLIAM'S
JOURNEY

United States
of America

A T L A N T I C

45°N.

30°N.

Bahamas

T R O P I C   O F

Cuba

Hispaniola

Puerto Rico

8

Jamaica

9

C A R I B B E A N   S E A

Leeward Islands

10

15°N.

11 12

Windward Islands

Barbados

7.5°W.

6.0°W.

4.5°W.

France

Sardinia

Corsica

Naples

MEDITERRANEAN SEA

O.1.2

3

4

Gibraltar

5

Sicily

Portugal

Spain

Algeria

Azores

Madeira

Morocco

6

O C E A N

Canary Islands

C A N C E R

Cape Verde Islands

500 miles

30°w.

15°w

0°

Francis Beaufort 1774-1857

Francis Beaufort was born in 1774, the son of an Irish parson. Being raised in an atmosphere of scientific curiosity, he was intrigued by mathematics and astronomy from an early age. These interests drew him to a naval career, in which they were essential to the all-important practice of navigation. In 1788 he made his first voyage onboard the East Indiaman *Vansitart*. Though shipwrecked while surveying a strait off Sumatra, the undaunted Beaufort returned home and joined the Royal Navy in 1790. He was made lieutenant in 1796. Four years later this promising career nearly came to an abrupt end when, boarding the Spanish brig *San Joseph*, he received two cutlass slashes, sixteen blunderbuss shots and a musket ball in his side. After a slow recovery he was given his first command in 1805, the supply ship HMS *Woolwich*. He sailed over 60,000 miles in her and gained a growing reputation as a surveyor of some distinction.

In 1812 Beaufort's active career finally did end when he was severely wounded by an angry mob while commanding the 32-gun frigate *Frederiksteen* on a mapmaking expedition to the coast of southern Turkey. He returned to England, where he published an account of the expedition titled *Karamania: A Brief Account of the South Coast of Asia Minor and the Remains of Antiquity.*

From this time onward, Beaufort worked tirelessly in the worlds of practical science and mapmaking, being given in 1829 the position to which he was uniquely suited, that of hydrographer to the Royal Navy. The 113 survey expeditions he commissioned produced 1,437 charts of hitherto little-known coastlines, and when he retired after 66 years of naval service, he left a legacy of accurate mapmaking that had a profound effect on the expansion of trade and marine safety. Even in retirement he pursued his customary practice of making daily weather records until three weeks before his death in December 1857.

Beaufort's plain, unfussy tomb stands largely unnoticed in the graveyard of St. John at Hackney, in the East End of London—curiously, a place in which he never lived. Buried with him are his first and second wives, and the one irretrievable blunderbuss shot fired by a Spaniard in 1800.

GLOSSARY

backstays: long support ropes from hull to mastheads, to counteract the force of the wind

bo'sun or *boatswain*: warrant officer responsible for the supervision and maintenance of the ship's sails, rigging, boats, etc.

brace: the horizontal adjustments of spars

chains: used to anchor the shrouds to the hull

clew lines: the ropes used to pull the bottom corners of a sail up to the center of the spar

close to the wind: with the wind just behind the sail

frigate: fast-sailing man-of-war

hydrography: the mapping of waters and coastal regions

jolly boat: the smallest boat carried by a ship as a means of transport from ship to shore—not considered lifeboats

jury rig: make-do mast replacing proper one—usually a spare spar or boom

knot or *nautical mile*: the distance of one minute or one sixtieth of a degree of longitude at the equator—1.153 land miles

larboard: now called port; the left side of a ship looking forward

leeside: away from the wind

mainsail or *course*: the lowest of the square sails—not found on the mizzenmast

man-of-war: warship

master: officer responsible for the day-to-day sailing of the ship—not the captain

midshipman: trainee officer

quarter: between abeam (at the side) and abaft (at the stern)

scudding: moving before a strong wind with little or no sail

sheets and *tacks*: the ropes securing the bottom corners of a sail

skid beams: large timbers crossing the open waist of the ship

starboard: the right side of a ship looking forward

storm staysail: fore and aft sail of heavier canvas set from the bowsprit

strike: take down to deck

topgallants: sails above the topsails used in lighter winds—next to topgallant mast

topgallant royals: very much fairweather sails, above the topgallants—next to topgallant royal pole

topsail: the most used sails—above the courses next to topmast

weatherside: whence comes the wind

yards, spars, booms: poles that hold the sails

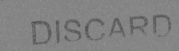